I0421908

THE BUSHCRAFT HANDBOOKS

FIREMAKING & LIGHTING

Illustrations by the Author

Richard H. Graves

The Bushcraft Handbooks
Firemaking & Lighting

This Edition Copyright © 2013 by Palmer River Publishing

Cover, Graphics and Layout by: Palmer River Publishing

ISBN-13: 978-1484842461
ISBN-10: 1484842464

About The Author

The author of "The Bushcraft Handbooks", Richard Graves, is a member of the Irish literary family of that name. A veteran of the Great War campaigns in the Dardenelles and the Western Front, the author became passionate about the bush at an early age. As an enthusiastic bushwalker, skier and pioneer of white-water canoeing, he foresaw how a knowledge of bushcraft could save lives in the Second World War. To achieve this end, he initiated and led the Australian Jungle Rescue Detachment, assigned to the Far East American Air Force. This detachment of 60 specially selected A.I.F. soldiers successfully effected more than 300 rescue missions, most of which were in enemy-held territory in New Guinea, without failure of a mission or loss of a man.

An essential preliminary for rescue was survival, and it was for this purpose that the notes for these books were written. These notes were later revised and prepared for a School in Bushcraft which has been operating for several years and continues to provide valuable instruction to Servicemen embarking overseas on active service in Korea and Malaya.

Bushcraft

As far as is known, "The Bushcraft Handbooks" are unique. There is nothing quite like them, nor is any collection of published bushcraft knowledge as comprehensive.

The term "Bushcraft" is used because "woodcraft" commonly means either knowledge of local fauna and flora or else is associated with the blood-sports of hunting and shooting. "The Bushcraft Handbooks" include a volume on traps and snares, but these are purposely-designed to be completely ineffective for native animals which are insect enters or grazers. These traps have been included because they would only be effective in catching predatory animals such as cats and dogs which have taken to the bush, and other "pest" creatures such as feral swine or goat.

"Bushcraft" describes the activity of how to make use of natural materials found locally in any area. It includes many of the skills used by primitive man, and to these are added "white man" skills necessary for survival, such as time and direction, and the provision of modern "white man" comforts as illustrated in the volume on bush campcraft.

The practice of bushcraft develops in an individual a remarkable ability to adapt quickly to a changing environment. Because this is so, the activity is a valuable counter to the over-specialisation so prevalent in today's society, and is particularly significant in youth training and character-moulding work.

INTRODUCTION to the BUSHCRAFT HANDBOOKS

THE PRACTICE OF BUSHCRAFT shows many unexpected results. The five senses are sharpened, and consequently the joy of being alive is greater.

The individual's ability to adapt and improvise is developed to a remarkable degree. This in turn leads to increased self-confidence.

Self-confidence, and the ability to adapt to a changing environment and to overcome difficulties, is followed by a rapid improvement in the individual's daily work. This in turn leads to advancement and promotion.

Bushcraft, by developing adaptability, provides a broadening influence, a necessary counter to offset the narrowing influence of modern specialisation.

For this work of bushcraft all that is needed is a sharp cutting implement: knife, axe or machete. The last is the most useful. For the work, dead materials are most suitable. The practice of bushcraft conserves, and does not destroy, wild life.

R.H.G.
April, 1952

CONTENTS

FIREMAKING & LIGHTING

The ability to obtain fire is essential in the bush. Fire can provide warmth, comfort, and protection. It is essential for the preparation of food, because heat in one form or another chemically affects the cells of plant foods, making some yield their nourishment, and others release their toxic elements.

Fire enables man to cook flesh and also to preserve it by smoking or drying. Fire is essential to make polluted water safe and drinkable.

The ability to obtain fire under any conditions, provided that combustible material is available, is one of the first essentials in out-of-door living.

The confidence which follows when one masters the skill of lighting fire with no equipment is remarkable.

Making fire by friction and other means is not easy, but when the skill has been mastered, the person acquiring the skill acquires greater knowledge of himself and greater confidence in his ability to overcome obstacles, both valuable characteristics in all avenues of life.

The ability to make fire under almost any condition is essential to the bushman.

It may be important, too, that you know how to make fire that is almost smokeless, or fire that gives little or no flame. In war these two conditions can be of the greatest importance. It is also important to know how to make fire for signals, so that if you are lost, rescuers can be guided to you, and, of course you need fire to cook your food, fire to warm you, and fire to protect you.

The Correct Way to Light a Fire with Matches

Even if you possess matches, lighting a fire in the bush may not be easy. The wood may be damp, it may be raining heavily, or there may be none of the usual aids, such as paper or kerosene. Therefore it is a good thing to learn how to light your fire with certainty under any condition.

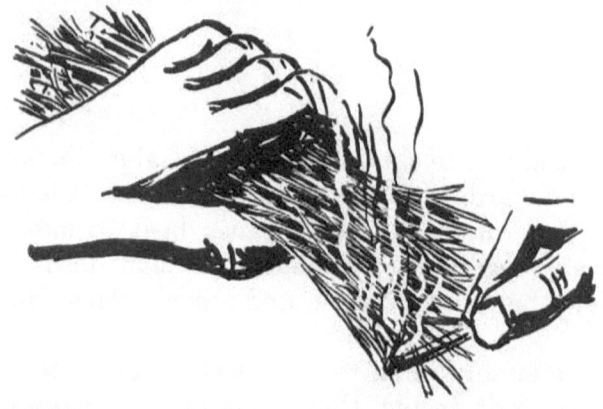

Unless the weather is very dry, and has been so for days on end, do not collect your kindling wood from the ground. It will certainly be damp, and in the morning, after heavy dew, wood picked from the ground will be far too wet to light. Acquire the habit of collecting the thin dead twigs, no thicker than a match, which you will find on almost every bush. Gather a big handful of these, and to start your fire hold the bundle in your hand, and apply the flame of your match to the twigs at the end farthest from your hand. They will catch fire easily, and you can turn the bundle in your hand until they are all well alight. Then lay the blazing bundle of twigs in your fireplace and proceed to feed other small twigs on top, gradually increasing the size until your fire is built to adequate proportions.

There will be occasions during very heavy rain when even the twigs are too sodden to catch alight easily. Then you must take a thick piece of wood, preferably from a branch which has not been lying on the ground, and with your knife, machete or tomahawk, split off the wet outer layer until only the dry wood inside remains. Shave this down in curls all round the sticks and make four to six such fire sticks. Hold these fire sticks by the butts in one hand and light the other end with your match. The dry curls will catch immediately, and the heat they generate in burning will be sufficient to during heavy rain you can light your fire with one match. In strong wind or during very heavy rain take your twigs, or fire sticks, inside your tent, and light them in the shelter so provided. Use your billy, carried on its side, to take the burning sticks to your fireplace.

These fire sticks, shaved from the inner wood dry after heavy rain, will take flame immediately. Four to six will start a fire for you.

Fire Without Smoke, and Fire Without Flame

As outlined in the first paragraph, there may be occasions when you desire to have fire without disclosing your position either through smoke or flame.

Smoke is the result of incomplete combustion, and therefore by ensuring that combustion is quickly completed the fire will be nearly all flame, with practically no smoke. This is achieved by feeding the fire with small dry twigs which catch alight almost instantly. By feeding the fire continuously with twigs 1/8 inch thick there will be no 'tell-tale' blue smoke haze. If possible light your smokeless fire under a tree (but not against the trunk); the leaves and branches will completely disperse what tiny amount of smoke is given off by the burning twigs.

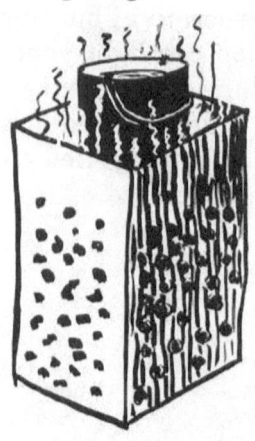

Fire without flame calls for the lighting of a small flame fire in the beginning, and then this is fed with charcoal, previously gathered from half-burnt stumps. It may be necessary to fan this continuously if there is no breeze. A charcoal fire needs a lot of air and, though it requires flame for starting, it will burn and give out great heat with a total absence of flame when well alight. An old kerosene tin or 4-gallon drum, pierced to allow plenty of air holes, makes a good brazier for a charcoal fire. By its use there is no visible flame. If a tin is not available, build a stone surround to your fireplace to hide the glow of your charcoal fire.

Lighting Two Fires with One Match at Different Times

To light two fires at different intervals of time with one match may appear to be impossible. But suppose you split one match? You then have two! and therein lies the secret of lighting two different fires with one match. There is a knack in splitting the match, be its stalk of wood, paper, or waxed fibre. There is also a knack in striking the split halves so that they will light, and there is also a knack in lighting your fire when the split match is aflame.

To split wooden matches, push the point of a pin or

a sharp knife immediately below the head, and force down sharply–the head will split in two and the wood run off or split. You have two heads and enough wood left on one half to burn for a second or more–long enough to start tinder blazing.

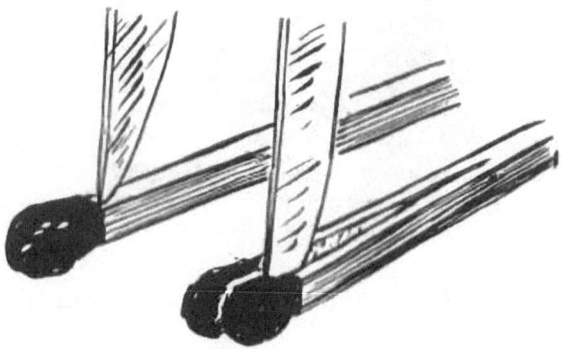

How to split a wooden match

With a paper match simply start to split the match at the end away from the head by peeling the paper towards the head. This will split the head, and so you have two matches, but each has a head on one side only.

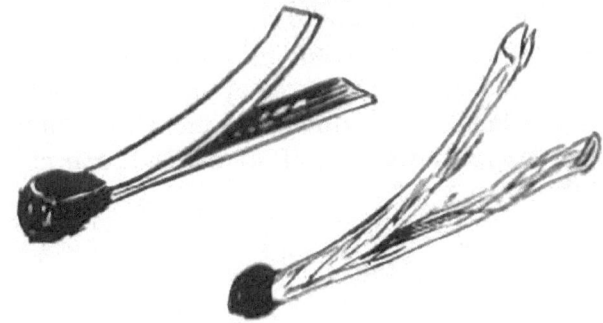

How to split a paper match

To split a wax match. Treat a wax match similarly. Split the match from the end away from the head and up to the head. It may be necessary to use a knife to split the actual head itself.

How to strike a spit match - draw flatly along box

In striking all three types of split match the 'stalk' of the match should be held between the thumb and forefinger, with the tip of the middle finger resting lightly on the head of the match. The match is drawn lightly and 'flat' along the striking surface. Immediately the head starts to burn, the forefinger which has been holding it gently down to the striking surface, is lifted and the match allowed to flame.

It requires practice to be certain that you can always split your match and strike both portions. (This splitting of matches reached a high degree of proficiency with prisoners during the Pacific war, and many men were able to split a match into six portions, and strike each one of them with certainty.)

Burnt Finger Cure

In learning how to strike a split match you will probably get a scorched fingertip on a few occasions. The quickest relief is to grab the lobe of your ear with the burnt finger. The natural oil on your ear will seal off the small burn from the air.

How to Prepare For Lighting Fire with a Split Match.

PRIMING

Lighting a fire with a single portion of a split match calls for extreme care in the preparation of your materials. A bundle of very thin dry twigs should be collected as for fire-lighting with one match, and the bundle should be loosely 'primed' in the centre with tinders of fine dry inflammable material, teased-out dry grass, a bit of teased cotton, fine dry teased-out bark or any of a hundred natural materials will do. Do not pack your tinder tightly or put in too much or you will 'drown' the tiny flame; just a very light priming will catch the flame quickly. When the little flame of the split match is applied to the tinder it must take the flame instantly and set fire to the thinnest of the dry twigs so that the whole bundle will soon be alight.

Lighting a fire with a split match should be practised in order to achieve real proficiency.

Keeping Reserve Matches Dry

Always keep a reserve of matches in your camp kit. These matches should be specially treated so that they are protected against wet. This can be done with ordinary safety matches by coating the head and stick with candle grease. Simply light a candle and drip the hot wax on the head, and rub some along the stick. The specially treated matches are best carried in a small screw-top plastic container. The striking side of a match box can also be wrapped in cellophane and enclosed in this container with the matches.

By preparing for sudden need through having this reserve of matches available you may save yourself much hardship and difficulty.

Lighting Fire From a Coal

Sometimes only a small red coal may be available to start your fire and, unless you know how, you will never get the coal to catch onto tinder, and so give you flame. It is important to know therefore how to make fire from a single tiny coal, no bigger than the pinched-out spark of a cigarette.

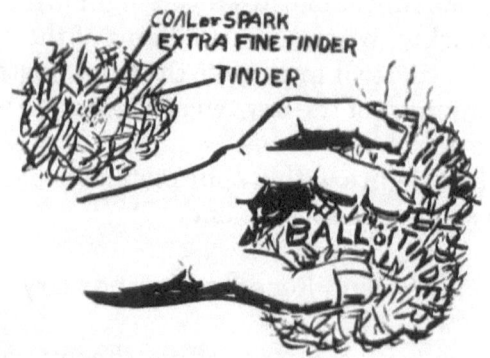

Lighting a fire from a coal.

To light your fire from a coal, collect a bundle of dry tinder (see 'tinders,'), softly tease a large piece, and place the coal in the centre, fold the rest of the tinder over the coal, and with the tinder ball held very loosely between the widespread fingers, whirl the ball round and round at arm's length, or, if there is a strong wind blowing, hold the ball in the air, allowing the wind to blow between the fingers. The ball will commence to smoke as the tinder catches. When there is a dense flow of smoke blow into the ball, loosening it in your hand. These few last puffs will convert the smouldering mass to flame and you will have achieved fire from a coal. This too should be practised frequently.

Firewood

Burning qualities of different woods vary greatly. Some such as pines burn with a clean bright flame and give out considerable heat.

Others char and smoke and give out little warmth.

In general all the pines burn well when dry, and most of the hardwoods are also good fuel, but there are a few species which are unsatisfactory for firewoods.

In tropical and sub-tropical areas, the soft woods of the rain forest are usually poor fuel, as are the trunks of palms, but palm leaves and stalks are good.

Trees which grow in swamp or marshland are rarely good for firewood.

The only way to know which species of wood in a locality are good fuel is to try and burn them. This will soon provide the answer.

In general, the firewood collected will be dead branches. Some of these will be on the ground, others still attached to the parent tree, or others possibly caught in shrubs beneath the tree.

It is better to collect wood from trees or shrubs, rather than wood which is actually lying on the ground. Wood picked up from the ground will usually be damp or even wet, but wood which has not lain on the ground will be comparatively dry, even in rainy weather.

For a fire for cooking, sticks half an inch to an inch in thickness are most suitable because the amount of heat can be controlled more easily.

For a fire for warmth, use thick logs. It will often be easier to burn a long log in half than to try and cut it. For these long logs, start the fire in the centre of the log, and when it burns through, the two halves will be easier to handle. For an all-night fire, occasionally pushing the two burning ends together will keep the fire burning gently, and a fair-sized log can be made to burn all night.

Cutting Firewood

The cutting of firewood into suitable lengths is always a worthwhile camp chore. Light sticks may be broken across the knee, and stacked in a pile by themselves. Heavier sticks can be broken in the same manner if they are first nicked deeply on opposite sides.

If the sticks are very thick they may be more easily broken by making deep cuts on opposite sides, and then hitting the stick down sharply on a convenient log or rock with the cut area at the point of impact. One sharp blow will generally break the wood, and you will be able to save yourself the work of cutting right through the wood.

The brittle, dead woods can usually be broken into short lengths by bringing the branch down in the above manner. Unless the wood is brittle enough to break off short it may jar your hands badly, so therefore it is advisable to try each piece lightly at first before you exert a full-strength blow.

Splitting Firewood

Blocks of wood are most easily split either around the circular rings (the round markings which show each year's growth), or radially, that is across the circular rings. Some woods will split easily either way. Others will be exceedingly tough.

If you try to split the wood the wrong way it will be very hard work and the wood will be 'cranky.' Immediately you try the right way the wood will split fairly easily, unless of course it is knotty. Trial and error is the best way to find out, and use a comparatively light blow to test the grain.

Breaking dead wood is easier than chopping.

When splitting wood with an axe blade the best results are obtained by driving the blade of the axe into the block of wood, then raising both axe and wood, and by reversing the axe head in the air, bringing the axe head down with the wood upermost. One blow in this manner will generally open the toughest block, provided it is not knotty.

After wood has been cut for the cooking fire it is good practice to stack it in graded heaps, little, medium, and big sticks separately, beside the fireplace, with fine twigs and thin slivers in a separate stack.

Woodshed

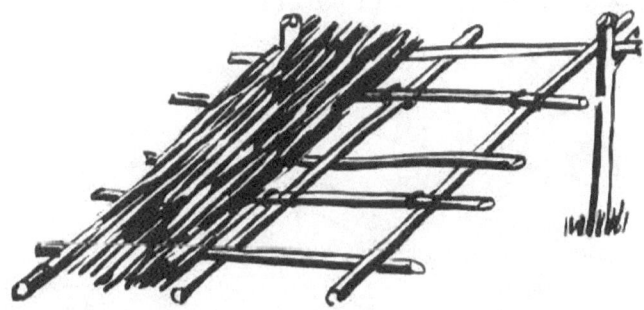

And finally, you will want to be prepared against a spell of wet weather, and so you'll need a small woodshed. Only then will there be a supply of dry kindling and wood after heavy rain.

The ground dimensions of your woodshed should be at least three feet by four, and about three feet high at the front. It should be to windward of your fireplace, so that windblown sparks will not fall on dry bark or other tinder.

Lighting Fire Without Matches

DIRECT FLAME - using sugar and permanganate of potash crystals, probably carried in the first-aid kit) mix together, and place in a hollow cut in a piece of dry wood. This hollow must be big enough to hold the whole of the dry mixture. Round off a straight stick, about 3/8 to ½" thick and 12" long to a shallow point. Place this end of the stick in the powder and rotate the stick rapidly between the two hands. The mixture will burst into a slow flame. Several attempts may be necessary to obtain ignition. This method may not be effective in damp or cold weather.

SPARK - Iron, iron pyrites and steel used with flint and also some of the very hard stones such as quartz will strike a strong spark, from which it is possible to get a spark for fire. The vital spark for fire-making may also be obtained by friction using a drill and bow, by a magnifying glass which concentrates the sun's rays, and by compression of air, which concentrates the heat. In the sequence of fire lighting without matches the first step is to get the spark, then from the spark to a coal and lastly from a coal to flame. The spark must be taken onto a tinder, and therefore the preparation of the tinder is a highly important part of fire-making.

Tinders and Their Preparation

The principle required from a tinder is that it must be readily combustible and finely fibred.

A simple test of natural, that is unprepared, tinder should be made to discover which materials are suitable. To make the test take a loosely teased handful of the material, place a coal from the fireplace in the material and blow. If the fire from the coal extends to the tinders it can be regarded as suitable.

Natural tinders are generally found in dry, beaten grass, finely teased bark, and palm fibre. Most of these coarse tinders are improved in their ability to take and hold a spark by being beaten and pounded until the fibres are fine and soft.

Natural fire-catching properties of tinders can be improved by the addition of a light dusting of very finely ground charcoal or, better still, by being thoroughly scorched.

If saltpetre is available a little may be mixed with the charcoal before it is added to the tinder, or the tinder itself can be soaked in a solution of saltpetre and water and allowed to dry out before use.

Tinder impregnated with a solution of saltpetre and later dried must be carried in an airtight container. If carried otherwise the saltpetre will become damp with moisture from the air. With this, or other prepared tinders you always have an emergency means of getting fire.

Old cotton or linen rag, scorched black and teased, is among the best of all tinders. A pinch of this, placed where the spark will fall, is certain to take the spark and quickly become a glowing coal.

Using these tinders, lighting fire from spark is comparatively easy.

Note. You will discover that some of the soft inner

barks, teased and spun into cord, will smoulder slowly when lighted. This is called a 'slow match.' It is worth while identifying the plants whose bark have this property. Lengths of cord made from such bark can be used to maintain a 'coal' for a long length of time, and so save your precious matches.

Striking fire from iron pyrites or quartz.

Striking a Spark

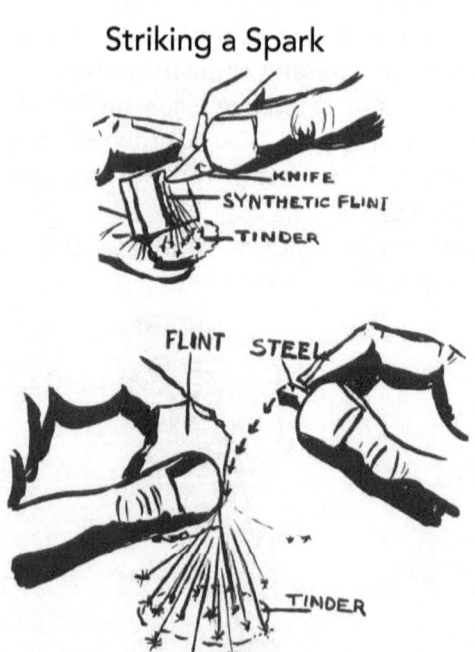

How to strike fire from flint and steel onto tinder.

Flint and steel, of course, were the common method of lighting a fire before friction matches were perfected and no great skill is needed for their use. The synthetic flint used in a cigarette lighter is a considerable improvement on natural flint. A couple of pieces of synthetic flint pressed into a small piece of 'perspex' make an excellent emergency firelighting outfit (heat the perspex and press the flints in while it is hot. Hold under cold water and the perspex will shrink on the flints and hold them securely).

An alternative to flint and steel are two pieces of iron pyrites, which, when struck together, throw off a shower of hot sparks that will last for at least a second. Iron pyrites is a common crystalline formation, and not difficult to obtain. Iron pyrites and steel will also give a hot spark. Quartz and steel, or two pieces of quartz, will also strike off good sparks, but these latter stones are very much harder to use.

The sparks struck must fall on the tinder, which, in turn, must be blown into a coal, and from the coal to a flame. Only a pinch of tinder is required when you are proficient with striking a spark.

Fire By Friction

Firelighting by friction consists first in generating a spark or tiny coal, and then nursing this (in the tinder) to flame.

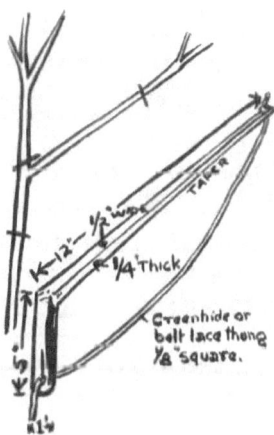

Bow. Thong is made from a leather lace or a strip of greenhide belt lacing.

15

Firelighting by friction is most easily mastered by the rotation of a drill or spindle in a foot piece. The drill, with some native people, is rotated between the hands but this requires considerable skill. Other primitive people rotated the spindle by means of a bow and thong. This last is the easiest method. The components, which should be prepared beforehand, are a bow, headpiece, drill, and footpiece. The dimensions given below are a guide for size.

To use a fireset, the drill is put under the thong, and twisted so that the drill finally is on the outer side of the thong, and with that portion of the thong nearest the handle of the bow on the upper side of the drill. This is important.

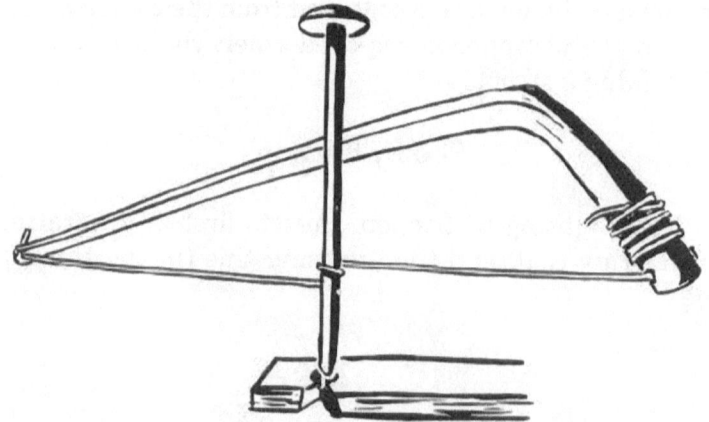

This is how the thong must be round the drill. If the thong is wrong way on the drill it will cross over itself and cut in a few strokes, also the full length of the stroke cannot be obtained.

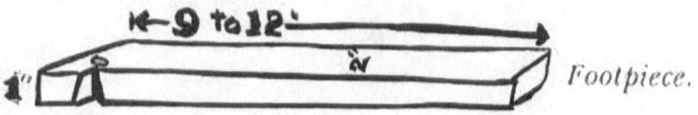

The foot piece has a shallow hole cut with a knife point into the upper side about half an inch from one edge. In this hole the drill is rotated. Into the edge of this hole from the nearest side, an undercut V is made.'This should be at least one-eighth inch into the hole itself.

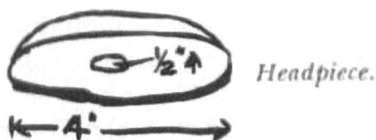

Headpiece.

The underside of the headpiece has a shallow hole bored into it, and this is lubricated preferably with lead (graphite) from a pencil. A smear of fat will also serve as a lubricant, or if even this is not obtainable, wax from the ear can be used.

The correct body position for using the bow .and drill is to kneel on the right knee, with the ball of the' left foot on the footpiece to hold it firmly to the ground. Place the lower end of the drill in the hole in the footpiece, and the top end of the drill in the hole in the underside of the headpiece.

The left hand holds the headpiece. The wrist of the left hand must be braced against the shin of the left leg. This will enable you to hold the headpiece perfectly steady. Actually the headpiece is a 'bearing' for the drill.

The bow is held in the right hand with the little and third finger outside the thong so that by squeezing these two fingers the tension of the thong can be increased.

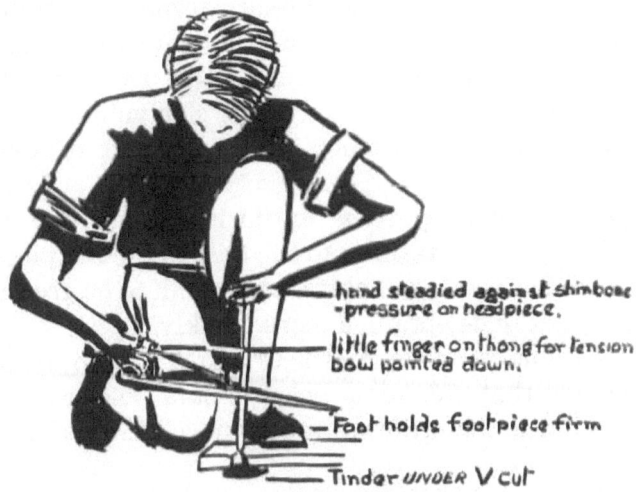

The correct position to hold the various parts of the fireset.

17

To learn to use a firebow it is advisable to learn first to rotate the drill slowly. This is done by drawing the bow backwards and forwards. The thong round the drill will spin the drill. Only a light pressure is put on the headpiece. Very soon you will see smoke coming from the footpiece, and notice that a fine brown powder is being ground out. This is forming a dark ring round the edge of the hole. This powder is called 'Punk.'

By examining it you can learn whether the woods you are using are suitable for firemaking.

The punk which will produce a glowing coal must feel slightly gritty when gently rubbed between the fingers, and then with more pressure it should rub gradually to a silky smoothness as soft as face powder.

This testing of the punk is extremely important. If you do not know for certain that the woods you are using are suitable for firelighting always make this test first.

When you consider that you have mastered control of the bow and drill you can start trying to get fire. Place a generous bundle of tinder under the V cut. When the drill is smoking freely and you have the 'punk' grinding out easily so that the V cut is full of it, put extra pressure on the headpiece and at the same time give twenty or thirty faster strokes with the bow. Lift the drill cleanly and quickly from the footpiece. Fold some of the tinder over lightly and blow gently into the V cut. If you see a blue thread of smoke continuing to rise, you can be sure you have a coal (you will probably see it glowing red). Fold the tinder completely over the footpiece, and continue blowing into the mass. The volume of smoke will increase, and a few quick puffs will make it burst into flame.

A tip given by some authorities is to put a little charcoal or gritty material into the hole in the footpiece. The claim is made that this enables more punk to be ground out, and the spark to be obtained more quickly.

Suitable woods for footpiece and drill, and this writer recommends that the same wood should be used for both parts, includes the willows and some of the non-resinous pines.

There are a few refinements which are worth knowing when you are making firebow set. These include the boring or burning of a hole for the thong at the tip and also through the handle of the bow. The end of thong at the tip of the bow has a thumb knot tied on the top side. The hole through the handle takes the long end of the thong, which is then wound round the handle in a series of half hitches. This hole in the handle enables you to adjust the 'tension' of the thong with greater accuracy.

A headpiece of shell or smooth grained stone with a hole in it is less liable to 'burn' than a headpiece of wood. Tinder should be carried in a waterproof bag.

Fire From a Magnifying Glass

Almost everyone at some time or other has focused the sun's rays concentrated by a magnifying glass (sometimes called a burning glass) onto a piece of paper or cloth to make it smoke. Lighting a fire with a magnifying glass calls for a ball of tinder with an inner core of extra fine material (see 'tinders,'). Onto this inner core the sun's rays are focused, and when the finer tinder is smoking freely, it simply requires blowing to produce flame. A concave mirror is even better than a magnifying glass. Powdered charcoal at the focal point will help the tinder take more easily.

Fire By Air Compression

In parts of Southeast Asia native people make fire by the ingenious method of suddenly compressing air in a cylinder and thereby concentrating the heat in the air to a point when the heat is sufficient to ignite tinder. (They did this hundreds of years before Dr. Diesel thought of the same idea for his engine.)

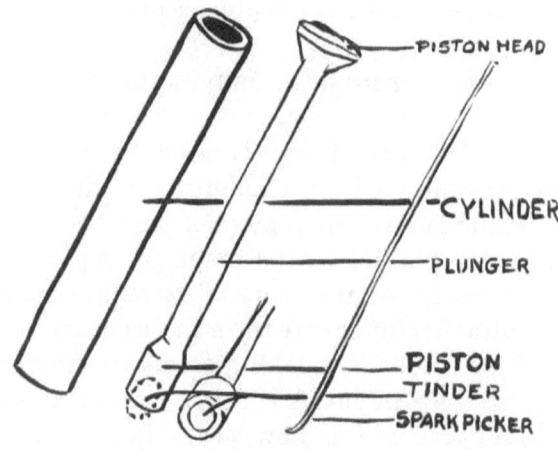

Their fire-making sets, frequently a cylinder of bone or hollow bamboo, with a bone or wooden piston, are almost museum pieces today.

In use a small piece of tinder is inserted into a cavity in the lower end of the piston. The piston is placed in the cylinder and the flattened end opposite the piston head struck a smart blow with the palm of the hand, driving it suddenly down the cylinder. Compression of air with concentration of the heat it carries produces a small glowing coal in the tinder placed in the recess of the piston head.' Frequently the jar of the blow will shake the tinder loose, so a 'spark remover' is used with the set to pull out the glowing tinder if it lodges in the cylinder.

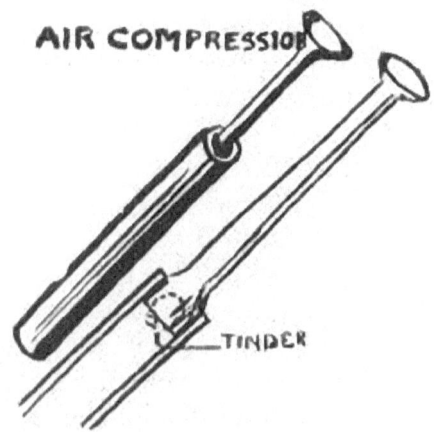

The dimensions are roughly as follows:

Cylinder. 4" to 6" long. Outside diameter ¾" to 1". Inside diameter about ½".

Piston. 4" to 6" long, of which the shaft is 3" to 5". Piston length ¾" to 1". Diameter–to nicely fit the cylinder.

Recess at lower end of piston-about ¾" wide by ¾" to 5/16" deep.

Piston shaft end is smooth and about 1" to 1½" diameter for striking with the palm of the hand.

Building a Fire

Combustion results when temperature is raised sufficiently high for the material to ignite. This is fire. Fire must have air, and you build your fire differently for different purposes.

For Cooking

A cooking fire must be a small fire, and one which is easily controlled. Often you need a 'long' fire because there are two or three billy cans, a griller and perhaps a frying pan, all of which must be on the fire at the one time.

Two green logs 6" or 8" thick placed about 12" apart will contain a cooking fire for you and make an excellent overnight fireplace.

A fire for cooking should be 'low,' with the quick heat of small wood. Too big a cooking fire will mean burnt fingers and burnt food. If the fire is too fierce, you will not be able to attend properly to the cookine of the food. There is a bush saying about cooking fires–'The bigger the fire the bigger the fool.' When laying a cooking fire it is a good plan to put a thicker stick in front of the fire. This will serve to rest your frying pan, and keep the heat from your hands; it will also help to contain the fire within the fireplace. A cooking; fire should always have a plentiful supply of small wood stacked conveniently near, so that you can feed the fire as the needs of the moment require.

The ideal way to build an open cooking fire.

In very windy or cold conditions it is worth making a reflector fireplace for your cooking. A few green logs placed as a windbreak to the windward side of your fire will enable you to do your cooking in comfort.

Fire in Flooded Areas

Fire can be made in areas totally covered with flood waters. The essential is to build a small platform above water level and on this light your fire.

The easiest way to do this is to cut four forked stakes. These must be straight along the line of drive with the fork projecting; from the side. They must be long enough for the fork to be about 6 to 12 inches above the level of water after the stakes are driven into the ground.

Across the forks at either end two cross sticks are laid, and on these two sticks a platform of other sticks is placed, side by side. These are covered with a couple of inches of mud, and on this the fire is built.

By extending the platform a foot or two at one end, you have a storage place for your firewood.

Fire for Warmth

If sleeping out without sleeping; bags or any bedding, select the site for your fire against a dead log. (But make sure the log is not a hiding place for snakes.) Rarely will a single log, burn by itself unless there is a strong draught blowing onto it; therefore you must feed the fire with at least one other log. This can be done by selecting a solid, fairly long log, eight or nine inches through if possible and six or seven feet long. By pushing the end of this against the bigger log where you have built your fire, you will ensure continued burning, and as the smaller log burns down during the night you can simply push it against the big log, and the fire will take fresh heart.

An alternative is to lay your logs like a star, and push the ends together during the night.

A small log pushed against a dead fallen tree will give you a good overnight sleeping fire. But be sure to put it out in the morning!

The Building of a Camp Fire

Solid Fire. Pyramid fire, lit on top.

This is the best of all campfires. Three or four logs about 3 ft. to 5 ft. long are laid side by side and across them another layer with, if you desire it, a third layer on top of these. On top of the top layer the starting fire is laid. This is built up finally like a small pyramid. This type of fire is lit at the top. The starter fire ignites the logs below with falling coals and so this fire burns downwards. It radiates heat evenly all round, and requires no attention during the night. Also, because there is no falling in of the fire the risk of sparks spreading and starting a bushfire is greatly minimised.

25

A common mistake in building a campfire is to make a 'pigsty' construction with heavy logs, on the outside and then pack the inside with light brushwood. Such fires are rarely a success. The light inside wood burns out in a quick blaze of glory, but the heavy outer logs lack sufficient heat to get them properly alight, and also having only small points of contact with each other at the corners do not burn well nor do such fires give out a good radiation of heat. If the 'pigsty' method is to be used, the top two layers should be completely across the top, one layer going in one direction and the other layer crossing it. These top two layers, when alight, get plenty of air from underneath after the brushwood has burnt out and the heat generated will be reflected downwards, giving better radiation than with a simple 'pigsty' construction.

"Pigsty" fire properly built.

Cone fire.

A good camp fire is built if the wood is standing end on, and the fire is built like a pyramid or cone. The centre is fired, and as the core burns away the outside logs fall inwards, constantly feeding the heart of the fire. This type of fire gives good radiation and even with wet wood burns well.

Slow Match

A slow match is a length of rope or cord which hangs in a smouldering condition to give fire when wanted. (ancient muzzle loading guns were fired by touching off the priming with a slow match.)

Today the slow match principle is used by many primitive people as a means of preserving fire and also as a means of carrying it from place to place.

A slow match can be made by making a length of cord or thin rope (from 1/8-inch to ¼-inch diameter) from suitable barks or palm fibres.

Most of the 'silky' soft-fibred barks are ideal. When one end is put in fire or against a glowing coal it will take and hold the spark, smouldering slowly.

A slow match is a safe way when you have no matches or fire-lighting material, to preserve the vital spark for further use after you have doused your fire and left camp for an hour or two. For such a use the slow match should be hung from a branch and exposed to the currents of air.

Fire in Wet Weather

The inclusion in your camp gear of firemaking aids such as a few Meta (dried alcohol) tablets is a matter of foresight which you will appreciate if you are overtaken by very bad weather.

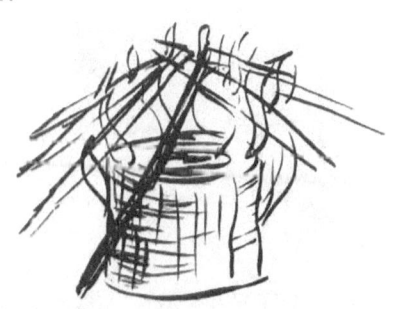

Kerosene-soaked Bandages

One of the really useful fire aids is a kerosene-soaked bandage. The kerosene does not affect the bandage—rather it acts as an antiseptic and helps keep the bandage sterile, and, if need arises, the kerosene-soaked bandage can be used to start a fire in very wet weather.

The best way is to pour kerosene into the roll of bandage until the roll is thoroughly saturated, but not to excess, or the 'dripping' stage. The bandage can then be put back again into the first-aid kit.

Fire Precautions

Observe these campfire rules and you will never start a bushfire.

NEVER LIGHT A FIRE AT THE FOOT OF A STANDING TREE OR TREE STUMP.

NEVER LIGHT A FIRE YOU CANNOT PUT OUT.

NEVER LEAVE A FIRE BURNING WHEN YOU LEAVE CAMP.

ALWAYS CLEAR AN AREA THREE FEET WIDE AROUND YOUR FIREPLACE.

Whenever possible, enclose your fire, either with stones, by using a pit fireplace, or by using a couple of green logs.

Bushfire Fighting

There are two main types of bushfires. Most frequent is a 'ground' fire in which the fire sweeps along the ground and lower growth, feeding upon the fallen leaves and grass and shrubs. The other type is a 'Tops' fire, in which the fire sweeps along the tree tops, the leaves of which, because of the intense heat, are rendered highly inflammable. Tops fires move with great speed, and because of terrific air currents which they generate, 'jump' considerable distances.

Most bush fires start as ground fires. When the weather is dry and hot, a ground fire can quickly grow to a Tops fire in heavily-timbered country.

Ground Fires

A ground fire can be fought either by beating it out or by making a fire break.

If the fire is purely a grass fire, use a green leafy branch to attack the fire by beating the burning edge back towards the burnt portion. When bush and low scrub are alight you may be able to beat the fire out with the green branch, but if

29

possible a length of sacking, thoroughly soaked, will prove a more efficient beater.

Beating out an extensive grass or scrub fire can be hard and difficult work.

If the fire extends along a wide front, too wide for you to attack, or if it is fanned by too high a wind, your best defence is to burn a firebreak between you and the approaching fire.

Select the line for the firebreak where the grass or scrub is thinnest and fire a small area–beating the young fire out on the side farthest from the approaching fire so that it will move away from you towards the main fire.

In the draught created by the heated air, the fire along your firebreak will advance against the wind, feeding upon the inflammable material in its path.

Extend your firebreak in a wide semicircle round the bush-fire side of your camp and when the approaching fire reaches the ends of your firebreak be ready to attack it if it starts to burn back against the wind.

Water, if available, can be used to fight a bushfire by playing a jet of water at the heart of the fire. The effect of water on burning wood is to reduce the temperature below combustion point.

"Tops" Fires

There is little that one or two people without firefighting equipment can do against a fire moving through the tree tops. The only really effective way to fight such a fire is by the cutting of firebreaks 100 to 200 yards wide–and this is impossible at short notice.

If a tops fire is approaching, the only safe place to take refuge is in a waterhole. It is no use trying to escape by running away from the fire. Men galloping in front of a tops fire on fear-maddened horses have been overtaken by the racing flames, which, in minutes, have killed both horse and rider.

Water Must Not Be Used on Oil Fires

If water is played on burning oil or fat the water particles are exploded and the oxygen and hydrogen of the water feed the fire, increasing its intensity and spreading the danger.

The only way to fight an oil fire is to seal the fire off from the air.

On one occasion the writer saw a forty-gallon drum of high octane petrol catch fire. It was one of a store of several thousand full drums. Everybody panicked and ran for cover except one man, who calmly walked over to the blazing drum, picked up a plug and sealed the opening. The fire went out immediately the air was cut off.

To fight an oil fire, throw sand or dirt on the seat, of the fire-that will seal off the air and the fire will die in a few moments.

This particularly applies to the danger of frying pans, where the hot fat catches fire—never ever throw water in the pan. Place it in a safe place where the fire can die down or throw dirt or sand or flour on the blaze.

Fire on Clothing

When clothing catches fire there is a tendency to panic and run. Keep calm—beat the fire out with the hands or roll in the dirt. Better still, grab a blanket or rug and roll in it. You may feel painful skin burns, but if you run, the air will feed the burning clothing and you may be so badly burnt that you will lose your life.

Water and Oil Fire

One of the hottest, most intense fires you can make is to burn water and oil together.

About the easiest method is to place a steel or iron plate on a couple of stones a foot above ground level. Light a fire beneath this plate to make it really hot and while it is heating up arrange a pipe or narrow trough about two or three feet long. One end of this pipe or trough is over the centre of the plate, and the other end is a foot or so higher than the plate. Into this top end of the pipe arrange, by means of a funnel and trough, water and sump oil to be fed down the pipe to the hot plate. The proportion of flow is two or three drops of water to one drop of oil. When the water and oil fall onto the hot plate it burns with a hot white flame of very great heat. The rate of flow can be governed by cutting a channel in corks which plug the bottles holding the water and oil, or if tins are used, piece holes in the bottoms of the tins and use a plug to control the flow.

This type of fire is excellent for an incinerator when great heat is required to burn out rubbish. It also makes an excellent 'Campfire' where strong flame and light are required and wood is in short supply.

FIREMAKING & LIGHTING

www.ingramcontent.com/pod-product-compliance
Lightning Source LLC
Chambersburg PA
CBHW050524290526
45786CB00007B/2690